Trey O'Brien

has reached the personal goal of

reading __10__ books in the 2005

We Dig Summer Reading Program

At the Stratford Library

Movement Adaptations

Animals have many ways to get from here to there.

Some animals move sideways to get across sand. Others make huge hops to look for faraway food. Some creatures even swing through the trees to escape from predators.

Find out how different animals get around and why they move that way.

Kangaroo

A booming, powerful bounce moves the kangaroo across the plain.

This animal jumps on strong hind legs. But the kangaroo uses more than just its legs to move around. Its huge tail helps the kangaroo balance during its long leaps forward.

Sometimes kangaroos have to search large areas for food. Hopping helps them travel for a long time without getting too tired.

Swing, Slither, or Swim

A Book About Animal Movements

by Patricia M. Stockland

illustrated by Todd Ouren

Special thanks to our advisers for their expertise:

Zoological Society of San Diego
San Diego Zoo
San Diego, California

Susan Kesselring, M.A., Literacy Educator
Rosemount-Apple Valley-Eagan (Minnesota) School District

PICTURE WINDOW BOOKS
Minneapolis, Minnesota

Managing Editor: Catherine Neitge
Creative Director: Terri Foley
Art Director: Keith Griffin
Editor: Christianne Jones
Designer: Todd Ouren
Page production: Picture Window Books
The illustrations in this book were prepared digitally.

Picture Window Books
5115 Excelsior Boulevard
Suite 232
Minneapolis, MN 55416
877-845-8392
www.picturewindowbooks.com

Library of Congress Cataloging-in-Publication Data
Stockland, Patricia M.
Swing, slither, or swim : a book about animal movements /
by Patricia M. Stockland ; illustrated by Todd Ouren.
p. cm. — (Animal wise)
Includes bibliographical references and index.
ISBN 1-4048-0933-3 (hardcover)
1. Animal locomotion—Juvenile literature. I. Ouren, Todd.
II. Title.

QP301.S84 2005
591.5'7—dc22   2004020802

5

Gecko

It turns upside down and back around. The small gecko can walk up and down any surface.

This little lizard can walk on walls and hang upside down from tree branches. Special toe pads help it climb and stick to almost any surface. Being such a good climber helps geckos reach food that other animals cannot.

Most geckos can even climb on smooth glass.

Bluefin Tuna

Fast fins swish and flutter as the bluefin tuna quickly swims by.

Tuna swims like most fish, with a side-to-side motion. The movement of its strong tail pushes the tuna swiftly through the deep sea. This fast-moving fish travels long distances across the ocean. It feeds on other fish along the way.

To go even faster, the tuna pulls some of its fins closer to its body. This movement helps streamline the fish.

9

Spider Monkey

A left arm, a right arm, and a tail go swinging by. The spider monkey swings through the trees.

Swinging from branch to branch is a great way to get fruit. The monkey's super-strong tail helps it hang upside down while holding on to supper. Staying in the trees keeps the spider monkey safe from predators.

The spider monkey's tail works like another arm. The underside is bare for extra grip.

11

Gazelle

Rapidly running across the plains, the gazelle quickly moves through the grass.

The gazelle is a very graceful animal. It is also very fast. Running helps these hoofed mammals get away from speedy predators such as cheetahs. Gazelles can also leap straight into the air when they are scared or surprised.

A gazelle's stiff leap is called stotting. Gazelles use this strange jump to warn each other of danger. The bounce means it's time to make a quick escape.

Sidewinder

Side-to-side wiggles move the sidewinder over the desert sand.

This rattlesnake doesn't move like other snakes. It presses its head and tail down, which moves it in a sideways motion. Then the sidewinder tosses itself to one side. Up goes the tail and over goes the snake, moving sideways across the sand.

Sidewinders live in dry, sandy deserts. It's easier for these snakes to throw themselves over the ground than to slide through the sand.

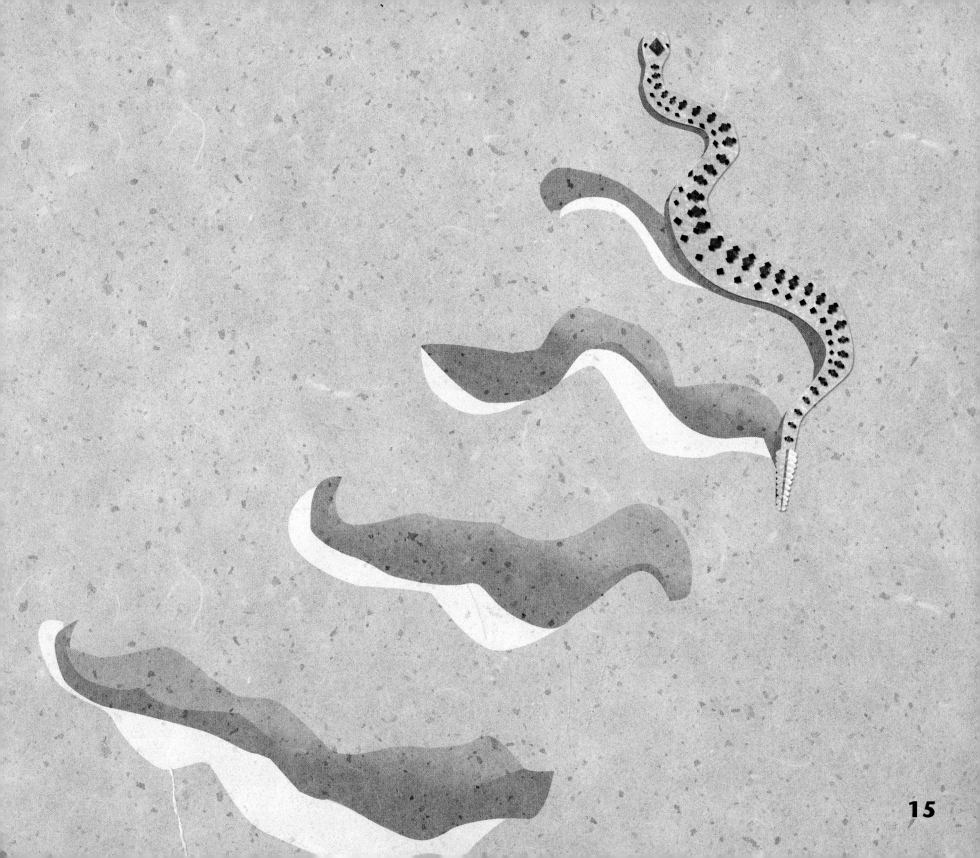

Jellyfish

First a big push, then a long glide. The jellyfish propels itself through the water.

The jellyfish moves by jet propulsion. First the creature fills its bell-shaped body with water. Then it squeezes the water back out. This strong push of water sends the jellyfish forward.

Some jellyfish float along the water currents rather than propelling themselves through the ocean.

Bat

It swoops, dives, and flies in the night. This little bat flaps its wings quickly.

The bat is the only mammal that can fly. Its wings are skin stretched between long fingers at the ends of their arms. Strong chest and back muscles help bats move their arms.

Some bats catch food while they are flying. Others, such as fruit bats, fly to reach their supper.

Penguin

It slides, splashes, and swims in the water. The penguin loves to play!

The penguin is a bird that doesn't fly. It waddles awkwardly on its feet. Sliding is faster and easier. The penguin slides on its stomach over the ice and snow. What a fun way to go!

Penguins move faster through water than on land. These black-and-white birds swim like dolphins, leaping in and out of the water to breathe.

Do You Remember?

Point to the picture of the animal described in each question.

1. I'm a mammal, but I can fly. My wings are skin stretched between my long fingers. Who am I?

   (bat)

2. I hop in long leaps across the plain. My big tail balances these bounces. Who am I?

   (kangaroo)

3. I swing through the trees to stay safe from my enemies. I also find fruit up here. Who am I?

   (spider monkey)

Fun Facts

For short distances, a kangaroo can hop at 30 miles (50 kilometers) per hour . That's as fast as a car on a city street.

Some geckos don't have eyelids. To keep their eyes wet, geckos lick their eyes with their tongue.

A spider monkey can cover up to 40 feet (12 meters) with one stride of its arms. That's as far as the length of a school bus!

Bluefin tuna can travel up to 5,000 miles (8,047 kilometers) while feeding. They travel in large groups called schools.

As bats fly around during the night, they can eat as many as 500 insects in one hour.

Glossary

current—water that is moving in a path, such as a river

jet propulsion—an action or motion that causes something to move forward

mammals—animals that are warm-blooded and have a backbone

predator—an animal that hunts and eats other animals

streamline—to make something smoother and faster

stride—a long, regular step

TO LEARN MORE

At the Library

Dell, Pamela. *How Animals Move*. Mankato, Minn.: Capstone Press, 2005.

Rose, Elizabeth. *Animal Adaptations for Survival*. New York: PowerKids Press, 2005.

Walker, Niki, and Bobbie Kalman. *How Do Animalss Move?* New York: Crabtree Publishing, 2000.

On the Web

FactHound offers a safe, fun way to find Web sites related to this book. All of the sites on FactHound have been researched by our staff. *www.facthound.com*

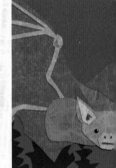

1. Visit the FactHound home page.
2. Enter a search word related to this book, or type in this special code: 1404809333
3. Click the FETCH IT button.

Your trusty FactHound will fetch the best Web sites for you!

INDEX

Look for all of the books in the Animal Wise Series:

Pointy, Long, or Round
A Book About Animal Shapes

Sand, Leaf, or Coral Reef
A Book About Animal Habitats

Stripes, Spots, or Diamonds
A Book About Animal Patterns

Red Eyes or Blue Feathers
A Book About Animal Colors

Strange Dances and Long Flights
A Book About Animal Behavior

Swing, Slither, or Swim
A Book About Animal Movements